Taking a breather in the Malvern Hills.

Most of us are familiar with commons. We may have played on them when young and visit them with our own children today. They can be places where we go to unwind from everyday pressures and exercise in the fresh air. Although immensely varied, they are often natural in appearance, with woods, hills and hollows offering opportunities to explore and observe wildlife. Many of us see commons as we travel each day, or as a view from our window. On holiday we may visit the vast commons of Wales, or of western and northern England, with their breathtaking views and exhilarating terrain. Millions of people visit common land each year. We can feel relaxed on commons, confident that we are entitled to be there.

Perhaps, because commons are so familiar, we may rarely consider what they really are, or how they came into being. When challenged, many people might think that commons are areas with no owner, or where everyone owns the land. Although legally neither statement is true (commons, like all other land, have an owner), it shows that many of us have close connections with commons, and indeed, neighbourhoods talk about 'their' commons and rightly feel entitled to a say in their future. This book examines how commons first became established, why they still surround us, and how we can ensure their survival for all to enjoy.

Commons in England and Wales

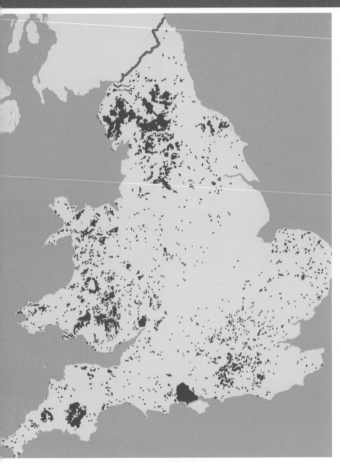

The common lands of England and Wales.

Commons extend from the windswept mountains of the Brecon Beacons ...

... to inner cities like Southampton.

Commons are found in all parts of the country, from the highest mountains to city centres. Nobody is ever far from a common. Yet now commons occupy just a tiny fraction of the area they once covered. During the Middle Ages common land was found extensively across Britain. At this time most fields, meadows, pastures, woods and even some wetlands were shared by local communities, at least for part of the year. Those areas of the country with better-quality soils and large rural populations were divided into tight-knit and self-sufficient communities called manors. The people within each manor would have enough land to grow their own crops, pastures to graze animals needed for meat and leather or to pull ploughs, a few meadows for hay, and woodlands to gather firewood and building timber. Nearly all of this was 'common land', meaning that it was shared and everyone could benefit. There was a lord of the manor, who had normally been granted the manor in exchange for undertaking certain tasks for the king, such as providing military service during times of war. Peasants would be required to work on the lord's private land (known as the 'demesne') during harvest and other periods. On the poorer soils outside manors there were extensive forests, which were also often commons. Manors and forests had their own local courts, which ensured that land was shared appropriately and nobody exceeded their common rights.

The commons found today are survivors from that time. There have been massive reductions in the area of common, as people with common rights have been removed, leaving private landowners in sole occupation – a process known as 'enclosure'. This occurred at various periods, including the 1200s, the mid-1500s, and especially during the main era of parliamentary enclosure in the 18th and 19th centuries. The loss of common lands for amenity and public enjoyment generated such a concern that it spawned Britain's oldest conservation charity, now called the Open Spaces Society, which spearheaded a national preservation campaign.

In England and Wales nearly all common land is mapped, either because it is registered under an act of parliament of 1965, or has its own legislation, like the New Forest and Epping Forest. In Scotland there is no similar legislation, although shared crofting land has many of the characteristics of common land. All the English and Welsh commons are now protected by law, and are also available for public access. Common land which may have once extended to half of England and Wales now covers less than four per cent. It is not distributed evenly. The biggest commons are on the hills of the Brecon Beacons, Gower, the Lake District, North York Moors, and south-western uplands like Dartmoor and Bodmin Moor. However, the largest numbers of small commons are found in south-east England, where, as at Hampstead Heath and Blackheath, they provide important recreational facilities for people from London and other major towns and cities.

Where Do Commons Come From?

The alignment of the great earthwork known as the Bokerley Dyke, which separates Hampshire and Dorset, also divides common land from arable, as it did in prehistoric times.

Common land derives from a time when a high proportion of resources were shared. The word 'common' comes from the Middle English term 'commune', with links to similar Old French and Latin terms, and indeed has roots in ancient Indo-European languages that are even older than Latin itself. The word effectively means 'general' or 'universal' – something that is shared. Human societies have always exploited a mix of shared and individual resources. Increasingly, western society has focused on exclusive property rights, where a person actually owns land, can exercise strong control over it and indeed determine whether anybody visits it at all. However, such a concept is essentially modern. Throughout much of history and probably prehistory, landscapes were shaped by complex relationships in which different rights, privileges and obligations were shared. Local people would hold and occupy but not own land, and in return had to undertake military or religious duties, or provide labour. Although some of our oldest acts of parliament relate to common rights, common land is older than legislation, and older than parliament itself.

There are commons that can be traced to the Saxon period, and the earlier layout of field patterns in Roman times hints at the presence of commons. Some commons may even be older. At Martin Down, a great bank known as the Bokerley Dyke, which now separates Hampshire from Dorset, also divides common land from arable fields. The same alignment shows a similar division of field systems and open grazing land in prehistoric times.

Sometimes new common rights were specifically granted, for example when the king gave monasteries and abbeys the right to graze their animals in royal forests, or when landlords granted rights to tenants. However, in many cases common rights became established gradually through custom and practice. Where people had exercised these rights for a significant time, they became recognised as entitlements. Even without legislation, such rights were protected by law. Local people would meet to consider the basis for rights and the rules for sharing resources, founded on custom and a concept of fairness. The words morality and mores (meaning 'custom') share the same Latin root. Rights did not normally belong to people, but were entitlements linked to properties. Even today, most common rights are exercised by people living at specified houses or farms. When the occupiers depart those properties, they leave the rights behind, and the new resident can exercise them.

In due course, local communities would keep a written record of their customs. At Minchinhampton in the Cotswolds, the customs of the manor were set down as early as 1299. These record the rights of different people to take stone, wood and fuller's earth (for cleaning woollen cloth), to graze animals and even to erect a cottage on wasteland. Alongside these rights, people also had specified duties, including haymaking, weeding, collecting nuts, looking after rabbits, lighting a candle in the chapel, and keeping a watch on St John's Eve (before midsummer) when spirits might rise from their graves.

Rodborough and Minchinhampton Commons in the Cotswolds, where the rights and duties of the local people were laid down in 1299.

Rights of Common

The right of pasture is still exercised by thousands of commoners today

Common rights are not held by the public in general, but are shared by particular people called commoners, who now have their rights registered. In England and Wales, over 36,000 common rights are registered. There are six main types that survive today:

Pasturage – the right to graze livestock

The right to put domestic stock onto common land remains important in many agricultural and rural economies. In many cases this relates to sheep, although entitlements to pasture cattle, horses or ponies are ·

also frequent. Very occasionally there are rights to graze goats or donkeys, or keep geese alongside rivers and ponds.

Estovers – animal bedding, sticks and wood

Deriving from an Old French word meaning 'necessary', estovers entitle people to take small wood (without felling whole trees) to repair buildings or make farm implements, collect firewood, or take bracken and heather for bedding and thatching. At one time rural communities were dependent on these rights to survive, but their importance has now declined.

Estovers – the right to collect sticks – was the main source of fuel for rural communities.

Pannage: pigs snuffling for acorns and beechnuts in the New Forest.

Turbary – cutting peat or turfs for fuel

These common rights are mainly associated with upland moors, and are recorded on 12 per cent of the Welsh and eight per cent of the English commons. Although peat-cutting is now rare, similar rights still provide a major source of fuel in parts of Scotland and Ireland.

Pannage – grazing pigs in woodland

The practice of fattening pigs on acorns or beechmast in autumn was widespread across much of Europe in medieval times. Certain woodlands in Domesday Book were valued according to the number of pigs they could support. The right is now exercised mainly in ancient royal hunting forests such as the New Forest.

Common in the Soil – taking minerals

This is a general term for an entitlement to take sand, gravel, marl, walling stone and lime from common land. The right is particularly localised in its distribution – for example, there is a cluster of such rights near Swansea. A particular form of common right to take coal and iron ore, known as free-mining, persists in the Forest of Dean.

Piscary – the right to take fish

Surprisingly, such rights are still found on 262 commons in Wales and England, although doubtless this is a tiny relict of a more extensive right formerly enjoyed.

Additional Rights

A number of other rights occur unevenly across England and Wales. An entitlement to take wild animals (*ferae naturae*) for personal consumption persists in a few places. Certain coastal areas of Norfolk have wildfowling rights. These sit alongside other peculiar entitlements, including a right to take seaweed, reeds (for thatching), shellfish, sea lavender and samphire.

In Norfolk there are common rights to take reed (for thatching), wildfowl, sea lavender, seaweed and samphire (Scolt Head).

Common Land and Farming

Bringing Herdwick sheep down from the hills in autumn, near Coniston.

Although all kinds of rights exist, it is farming, or more specifically the use of rough pasture by sheep, cattle and other domestic stock, that created most of the common land found today. These animals control vegetation, prevent land from becoming overgrown, and maintain the special landscapes enjoyed by so many people. Whereas commons were once the lifeblood of country communities, there are now just a few thousand farmers who exercise their rights. It is in the uplands, on the unfenced expanses of places like the Brecon Beacons, North York Moors, Lake District and Dartmoor, that commons remain central to rural land-use. Common pasture provided the products that people needed to survive, including meat, milk, cheese and wool. It also ensured grazing for draught animals for pulling ploughs and carts, and manure for fertilising fields. Today, commons still provide an environmentally-friendly source of meat from land kept largely free of chemicals.

Hill farmer Carl Walters on the enormous Bampton Common in the Lake District.

On the large upland commons, sheep flocks from each farm generally occupy a defined territory. This is often called a heft, or sometimes 'heaf' or 'lear' in parts of England or 'cynefin' in Wales. These hefts were initially formed by shepherds pushing back wandering animals onto familiar ground. Once hefts are established, generations of lambs learn the bounds from their mothers. Hefting can be critical to farming, making it more practical to gather sheep on the hills, and preventing straying animals getting into difficulty on dangerous cliffs, in bogs or entangling vegetation. In some cases hefts are hundreds of years old.

Not only do neighbouring farmers share commons, but they often need to work collaboratively on the land when gathering stock or controlling disease. In the uplands, trained sheepdogs are vital to farming, and particular breeds, capable of rounding up distant animals and responding to calls and whistles, are favoured depending on the terrain and conditions. Sheepdog trials, shepherds' gatherings and other communal activities help engender the neighbourliness essential to successful hill farming.

Most commoners have fields or 'inbye land' close to their farms, where grazing, supplementary feed or housing can be provided at critical seasons of the year, animals can calve or lamb, and they can be sorted or treated. This leads to a characteristic landscape of small valley fields and settlements, with great unbounded uplands.

Many specialised breeds of stock are associated with commons. These have been selected for their ability to thrive in the difficult climate and rough terrain of many commons. For example, Herdwick sheep are largely confined to the Lake District and Yorkshire Dales, where their hardiness and strong hefting instincts have made them important components of hill farming. Exmoor ponies, the breed most closely resembling the original European wild horse, are closely associated with common land. The survival of hill farming is critical to the conservation of common land. In those areas where commoning has died out, the land can revert to scrub, lose its wildlife and become inaccessible.

Shepherds' gathering at Borrowdale.

The relationship between shepherd and dog is central to sheep farming on upland commons.

The Struggle Against Enclosure

Mousehold Heath today, where 15,000 commoners gathered before seizing Norwich

Enclosure (often spelled 'inclosure' in older documents and acts of parliament) is the name given to the legal process through which common rights are terminated and common land converted to the exclusive property of the landowner. Unsurprisingly, the removal of people from the land sometimes generated unrest.

The greatest incident occurred in Norfolk in 1549, when the country was unsettled by high rents and widespread evictions. The distinction between rich and poor became dangerously wide. Landowners acquiring properties from the disbanded monasteries sought to exclude commoners, and far-reaching disturbances threatened to erupt into civil war. In Norfolk fences symbolised oppression by a powerful elite.

Paradoxically, the leaders of the Norfolk uprising, Robert and William Kett, were landowners themselves who became sympathetic to the commoners' plight. They offered to lead a march to Norwich in defence of common rights. News spread quickly, and by the time they camped at Mousehold Heath, a great common outside Norwich, they were 15,000 strong. Anxious to dissipate unrest, the king offered a pardon, which the rioters rejected, claiming that they had committed no crime.

The Ketts' army then seized Norwich. A contingent of 12,000 professional soldiers and mercenaries, including cavalry and artillery, forced the rebels back to Mousehold Heath. In the final battle, 3,000 weakly armed rebels were slaughtered and those fleeing were

The Abbey at Wymondham, where the Norfolk rebellion started and William Kett was hanged from the west tower.

mercilessly pursued. Robert Kett was hanged from Norwich castle, his body left to rot, while William was suspended in chains from Wymondham Abbey, thus turning a house of religion into a place of execution. The Norfolk rebellion widened the gulf and class divisions between lord and peasant.

Riots also erupted alongside parliamentary enclosure. The normally tranquil basin of Otmoor in Oxfordshire was the scene of legendary uprisings. Its 4,000 acres of marshland had been used as pasture by seven surrounding villages since time immemorial. Wealthy landed interests were able to get an Enclosure Act in parliament. However, it was not until a new drainage channel accidentally flooded adjoining land that direct action was taken: men tore down the embankments. At their trial, they claimed that they were simply relieving their lands of a public nuisance and were acquitted. Buoyed by this news, the people of Otmoor concluded that the fences were similar nuisances, and might be removed. Up to 100 men with blackened faces, summoned at night by the blast of a horn, gathered and destroyed fences. With increasing resolve, an estimated 1,000 villagers then beat

the bounds of their common, a distance of seven miles, in broad daylight, proclaiming 'Otmoor for Ever', and broke any remaining fences. The police were impotent to control the numbers and summoned military support. Prisoners were taken in wagons to Oxford castle, but a crowd at St Giles's fair overcame the troops and released the captives.

Resistance on Otmoor continued for five years. In the end, though, the commons were lost, and the poor made poorer. Through the enclosure award, only 73 people of a population of 1,700 were granted any land at all, and the majority got just five acres. The great beneficiaries were the Oxford colleges, clergymen, the Duke of Marlborough and Earl of Abingdon.

Robert Kett rousing supporters under the great oak at Wymondham, as depicted on the town sign.

Turning the Tide

Thirlmere in the Lake District, whose flooding to provide a reservoir for Manchester helped strengthen the environmental movement in Britain and establish the National Trust. © Paul McGreevy

Although enclosure enabled intensive food production for a growing urban population, and made many landowners wealthier, the burden of poverty fell hardest on those commoners who were least able to endure it. The elimination of the commons escalated in the early 19th century, as the parliamentary process was cheapened and simplified. Following an act of 1845, the process of enclosure could be completed in just two or three years, and six million more acres of common land were removed. However, the loss of commons and the stopping-up of paths had generated riots in many places. As a minor but significant concession, the 1845 act required the health, comfort and convenience of local people to be considered during enclosure, and certain modest allowances were made.

Peasants with a few livestock had been inadequately organised to make their collective voice heard amid powerful interests. Nevertheless, a growing public appreciation of the countryside by holidaymakers, and recognition of the importance of green space for the health, contentment and well-being of cramped city-dwellers, generated a burgeoning social movement. In 1865 things came to a head. The need for more building land, coupled with claims that many of the London commons were unkempt wastes, suffering from tipping, gypsy camps and insalubrious behaviour, enabled landowners to propose major development schemes. There were plans to build across Putney Heath and Wimbledon Common, and 1,000 acres of Epping Forest were felled.

A parliamentary committee heard evidence from those concerned about the loss of amenity. The MP George Shaw-Lefevre (later Lord Eversley) was so concerned that he went on to found the Commons Preservation Society (now the Open Spaces Society). This lobbied for and secured a new act in 1866, which enabled commons in London to be regulated. This was a far-reaching event because it showed that commons were important to the public as a whole, alongside those with common rights. Meanwhile, the formerly all-pervasive power of lords of the manor was severely curbed. Wimbledon Common, Hampstead Heath and Epping Forest were saved for the nation.

Initially it was unclear whether the society would be solely London based, but an enclosure riot at Fakenham in Norfolk was instrumental in transforming the society into a national body. The Commons Preservation Society worked by galvanising public interest and lobbying the government using eminent and influential supporters, but it also took direct action where necessary. Following the enclosure of 400 acres of Berkhamsted Common, Hertfordshire, in 1866, in co-operation with Augustus Smith, the society sent 120 labourers from London, who worked by moonlight to dismantle the fences and save the common.

Although it managed to secure certain public access, the society was unable to halt the flooding of Thirlmere valley in the Lake District in 1879 to make a reservoir for Manchester. The society's secretary, Robert Hunter, and two of its committee members, Octavia Hill and Canon Rawnsley, realised that there was a need to establish a body capable of actually owning land, in order to protect it fully. Hence a new body, the National Trust, became established within the very offices of the Open Spaces Society.

Above: The common of Hampstead Heath was saved from development at the eleventh hour.

Below: Berkhamsted Common in Hertfordshire, where the Commons Preservation Society (now Open Spaces Society) organised a party of 120 labourers to remove fencing on the common.
© Paul Downey

Cowherds' or Cowards' Marsh in Dorset, in winter flood

Those commons that survived the enormous pressures of enclosure in the 18th and 19th centuries often did so for specific reasons. The most productive commons were enclosed first, meaning that those with more difficult terrain sometimes endured until the national outcry for protection turned in their favour.

The majority of the surviving commons are on hill land with poor, stony or peaty – and sometimes waterlogged – soils. These often have dramatic scenery, command expansive views, and are exposed to severe weather with challenging conditions for visitors. They consist of open moorland with heath and bog vegetation, and are exceptionally important for wildlife. They are used by common right-holders for rearing hardy sheep breeds like Swaledale and Welsh Hill Speckled.

Some commons, such as those in the Avon Valley near Christchurch, Dorset, flood in wet winters, making agricultural improvement costly and risky. Such inundation helps prevent the flooding of nearby settlements, and also supports a wide range of waterfowl. Cowherds' or Cowards' Marsh has an ancient, highly regulated system of hay-cutting, grazing and resting, with a resident marshman. Townspeople were permitted to turn out two 'rother' beasts (horned cattle) when the site was 'breached' after hay-cut, alongside celebrations at the Marsh Fair. From Lammas Day (1 August) the site was rested, although in drier winters animals could be returned until Candlemas (2 February). Local people were also able to collect bundles of gorse as fuel. Some coastal commons in East Anglia, with grazing marshes and reed beds criss-crossed by creeks, can be submerged by exceptional tides, and this has similarly helped protect them from agricultural improvement.

The New Forest was common land when it became a royal hunting forest in 1086 and remains common land today.

Watendlath in the Lake District, where the terrain and weather severely restrict land use.

In certain cases unusual legal provisions have prevented change. The New Forest became a royal hunting forest under William the Conqueror, although it was already common land at that time. Commoners today still put out thousands of cattle and ponies, with some pigs and donkeys, which maintain the character of the open forest. The area is partly under the control of Verderers (a Norman word linked to 'vert' or greenery), who manage the commoning on which the New Forest's landscape depends. The area is a national park and has millions of visitors each year.

The environmental importance of many commons has led to them being acquired by the National Trust, Wildlife Trusts and local councils, who manage them for conservation and amenity. In some cases action by pressure groups, like the Open Spaces Society, has ensured commons have survived.

Paradoxically, some commons derive from the time of enclosure itself, when small parcels known as 'poor's allotments' were established for local people to gather fuel when all their other resources were being lost. These relics are now often the sole indicators of formerly extensive landscapes.

Access

An estimated 16 million people visit the Lake District each year, in all seasons: Harrison Stickle.

People have a right of access on foot (with special provision for disabled people) to virtually all common land in England and Wales. Although some commons have been used as amenities for centuries, it was not until the year 2000 that a formal right in law (the 'right to roam') was conferred on all such land. Now people can enter and remain on commons and other access land for as long as they like, 'for the purposes of open air recreation'. Such areas are shown in yellow wash on Ordnance Survey Explorer maps. Unlike the situation on rights of way, where people are confined to paths, members of the public can go where they choose on common land, off the beaten track. Provided that they act responsibly, respecting farming interests and the welfare of livestock, they can hike, picnic, play, watch wildlife or climb. The rights do not extend to the use of vehicles (including bicycles), horses, metal detectors, hang-gliders or to camping (where normal permission would need to be sought). This law gives formal recognition to the reality that commons have become increasingly important to the wider visiting public, in addition to the local communities that they serve. Now some 398,000 hectares in England and 175,000 hectares in Wales can be visited and enjoyed.

On certain commons, in addition to access on foot, there are wider rights to 'fresh air and exercise'. This includes horse-riding, but does not permit vehicles, camping or lighting fires. These wider rights often apply where commons once came within an urban district or borough, or because of special laws and provisions. It is not always easy to tell whether such rights exist, and it is best to check local information.

Commons are found in all areas so they constitute a substantial recreational resource. Our largest commons are found in the uplands, and cover some 430,000 hectares, an area greater than all but a few English counties. Their unfenced landscapes convey a sense of remoteness and grandeur. Nearly half of all common land is found in our national parks. The Lake District, Dartmoor and Brecon Beacons contain extensive common land, whilst two-thirds of the New Forest is common. Each of these has millions of visitors each year, who contribute to the local tourist economy.

There are also thousands of commons accessible to people who live in urban areas. The commons of the Gower Peninsula, including the coastline of Rhossili and the hills of Cefn Bryn, are not only popular destinations for holidaymakers, but within easy reach

of ten million people. But the greatest numbers of commons are found in south-east England. Surrey has over 9,000 hectares, including the nature reserve of Chobham Common which has a quarter of a million visitors per year. There are 120 in London, including Hampstead Heath. Despite their location, city commons can retain the wild appearance that reflects their origins, providing a refreshing alternative to more manicured parks and gardens.

Woodgreen, Hampshire. Additional access rights for the use of horses or bicycles exist on some commons.

City break – Southampton Common.

Wildlife of Commons

Golden plover, whose eerie cries echo across moorland commons in summer.

The uncommon Adonis blue butterfly on a limestone common in the Cotswolds.

The English and Welsh commons are free from farm chemicals like pesticides, herbicides and artificial fertilisers, and have soils which have been undisturbed for centuries, so they are brimming with wildlife. In fact, they probably support a more diverse flora and fauna than any other type of farmland. Much of the wildlife found on common land is dependent upon traditional grazing by livestock, which controls scrub and coarse grasses, and keeps sites open to sunlight and suitable for a wide variety of species.

About half of all common land comprises heath and moor on acid soils. These are covered with low shrubs, especially ling and bell heather, cross-leaved heath and myrtleberry. Such conditions provide good cover for ground-nesting birds, mammals and reptiles. However, commons include a wide range of other habitats, such as saltmarshes, sand dunes, woods, wetlands, mountains, bogs and lowland grasslands. Chalk and limestone downs are especially rich in flowers, with dozens of species growing closely together in a short sward.

Such downlands are spattered with colour, ranging from the electric blue of milkwort and pale sulphur of cowslips, to the pink of rest-harrow and sanfoin. Common land supports many showy orchids – there are nine different types found on the Cumbrian commons alone. Strong-smelling herbs like wild thyme and marjoram can also conspire to produce an intoxicating atmosphere on warm days.

Such areas are buzzing with insect life during summer, with clouds of butterflies and day-flying moths erupting from each footfall, and the chirrup of grasshoppers and crickets. Several spectacular butterflies are associated with lowland commons, including the local marsh and dark green fritillaries, and the Adonis blue whose caterpillars feed on horseshoe vetch.

Upland peatbogs and moors provide important territories for uncommon breeding waders, like golden plover, whose plaintive calls haunt the hills in early summer, together with those of curlew, lapwing and snipe. Birds of prey, including peregrine, merlin and hen harrier, are also strongly linked to upland commons. In contrast, the lowland heaths have important populations of the scarce nightjar, whose throaty, nocturnal chirring can be heard hundreds of metres away, together with woodlarks and Dartford warblers, which, unlike nearly all their close relatives, stay in Britain during the winter. Warm lowland commons are also particularly important for reptiles and amphibians, including the nationally-rare sand lizard and smooth snake. Some areas of coastal common support massive populations of

waterfowl in winter, with thousands of geese forming great noisy flocks which gather to roost at sunset.

Spatters of mixed colours characterise chalk-downland commons in summer.

Noisy geese returning in their thousands to coastal commons in Norfolk at a winter sunset.

Archaeology and Commons

This cleft marks the site of a Neolithic axe factory at Pike Stickle, where polished greenstone axes were made and transported across Britain and Ireland.

The archaeological monuments found on common land span the 12,000 years since the last ice age, and range from flint workings, stone circles, hill forts and settlements, to military sites and gold mines. There are tens of thousands of such sites safeguarded on the unploughed soils of commons, which elsewhere have been obliterated by modern agriculture. On those commons near the heart of major towns and cities the archaeological features have been protected from development.

For example, Port Meadow in Oxford preserves six Bronze Age barrows and three Iron Age farmsteads.

Some of the upland commons, such as those in south-west England and the mountains of Wales, have so many monuments that they reveal how whole landscapes have evolved over millennia. Dartmoor alone has over 450 listed archaeological features. It has the largest assemblage of stone rows in Britain, with at least 75 examples, some of which exhibit links to similar monuments in northern England and Brittany. Massive standing stones, up to four metres high, form the terminals of rows at Drizzlecombe on Dartmoor, in a setting littered with Neolithic enclosures, roundhouses, massive stone cairns, a stone circle, and the extensive remains of more recent tin mines, suggesting thousands of years of occupation.

Where ancient pollen, charcoal, animal bones, snail shells and beetles have been preserved alongside archaeological features, information can be gleaned about the vegetation and conditions present when such monuments were constructed. Some abandoned hill farms also shed light on the different climates that prevailed in certain prehistoric periods. For example, the remains of Bronze Age settlements which are now found in the inhospitable, wet and cold conditions of the Berwyn in Wales have small fields alongside, which were once capable of growing crops.

Certain archaeological features suggest that commoning itself may be thousands of years old and was perhaps universal throughout Britain. Farming hamlets which were occupied in the Bronze Age have groups of roundhouses with separate fields, between which are walled lanes suitable for moving livestock. These lanes broaden as they approach the surrounding open moorland, suggesting that animals were frequently driven from the moor, perhaps for protection or milking. Such a layout closely resembles commoning farmsteads surviving today. In some cases settlements were probably occupied only seasonally, with animals being driven there to take advantage of summer pasture; at Perfedd in Ceredigion there may have been 50

summer shepherding stations. The size of monuments also reveals something about the landscape at the time when such features were built. At Leskernick in Cornwall there is a stone row barely projecting above the ground. This suggests that it must have been built in a landscape with very short vegetation, perhaps resembling the one persisting today.

Massive standing stones mark the ends of the Drizzlecombe stone rows on Dartmoor.

Hardknott Roman fort, controlling a high mountain pass in the Lake District.

Folklore and Customs

Great Wishford villagers at Salisbury Cathedral celebrating their common right to take green oak from Grovely Wood.

Commons are ancient components of the landscape, so it is not surprising to find many customs associated with them. These traditions would have helped an illiterate community preserve their rights through collective memory, similar to walking around the edge of the parish each year to remember the boundary features – often called 'beating the bounds'.

Before dawn on Oakapple Day each year, the inhabitants of Great Wishford in Wiltshire are woken to shouts and the clashing of dustbins as they are beckoned to climb into Grovely Wood to collect green oak boughs. The villagers are celebrating common rights which go back more than 500 years. They suspend the boughs from their church (also using them to bless newly-weds) and decorate the village prior to festivities. Sticks are gathered into 'knitches', an ancient term for small bundles, and taken to the green at Salisbury Cathedral, where knitch-ladies perform a dance. Inside the cathedral, villagers read a charter asserting their common rights, and then they beseech all onlookers to take part in their cry of 'Grovely Grovely and All Grovely'.

Written records of these customs survive from the 1500s. They state that villagers have by 'ancient custom' the right to fell one cartload of trees pulled only by manpower each year. They can also gather and bring away all kinds of 'dead snapping wood' and sticks at their pleasure 'without controlment'. The records relate how 'since ancient times' the villagers have gone in a dance to the cathedral and made claim to their custom in these words: 'Grovely Grovely and All Grovely'. The charters show that these customs 'are rights, have always been rights, and ought to be rights'. In 1597 they were described as 'old and ancient customs' and 'time out of mind'. However, the dance, in its current location, cannot have been performed earlier than the building of Salisbury Cathedral in 1220.

Common rights were normally controlled alongside other matters in the local manor court, in which many right-holders would form part of the jury. Most local courts had fallen into abeyance by about 1900, but there are a few that still meet, such as at Wareham in Dorset and Stockbridge in Hampshire. New commoners on Danby Common in the North York Moors still have to be sworn in at Danby castle.

Many customs are associated with the rearing of livestock. Unique lug (ear) marks used for sheep in the Lake District may have Viking origins. Sheep counting using the numbers yan, tan, tethera, methera, pip (for one to five) can be found in a variety of forms throughout the country; the language is linked to Welsh and Cornish, and derives from Celtic dialects used before the Saxon invasions.

The meadsman of Pixey and Yarnton Meads, Oxford, with the wooden lots which have been used to allocate hay-strips since the Middle Ages.

At Pixey and Yarnton Meads, beside the Thames near Oxford, there are lot-meadows where, through ancient custom, each person's allocation of hay was determined by drawing cherry-wood balls from a bag. The practice may be older than the Norman Conquest. The balls bear names traceable to families present in the Middle Ages. The hay all had to be cut in a single day, using travelling labourers, and was followed by boisterous celebrations, much to the dismay of the local clergy.

Commons in Literature

Brendon Common on Exmoor in Devon provides the setting for *Lorna Doone*.

Commons were part of the everyday experience and therefore they feature prominently in the arts. Brendon Common on Exmoor forms the 17th-century setting for the romance and fighting in R.D. Blackmore's *Lorna Doone*. Many writers, such as Oliver Goldsmith, George Crabbe and Thomas Hardy, championed the plight of the rural poor. However, it was John Clare (1793–1864), the peasant poet from Northamptonshire, who more than anyone lamented the loss of commons and the poverty that ensued.

Clare, a shepherd and farm labourer, was 27 when an enclosure award spread dramatic change through his community. As his beloved landscape was obliterated, he was disorientated, commenting that with the cutting down of the last elm, 'all the old associations are going'. Of particular significance was Langley Bush, a wide, low mound south of Clare's village of Helpston, which sported an old thorn tree. The raised ground, perhaps derived from an ancient tumulus, had been a prominent landmark for centuries. It lay beside a Roman road, marked the junction of three parishes, and according to folklore once held a gibbet (criminals were often executed at boundaries, on the edge of society). The site was first recorded in Saxon times, and even then was marked by a 'common thorn'. Clare described how he often made journeys over the heath to experience 'the shepherds' sacred shade'.

As waves of agricultural improvement swept through Northamptonshire, Clare wrote, 'last year Langley Bush was destroyed. An old white-thorn had stood for more than a century, full of fame, and the Gypsies, Shepherds & Herdsmen all had their tales of its history.' In his poem, Clare bade farewell to the bush, 'Like an old companion ne'er to meet again'.

In his poem 'The Mores', Clare bewails the carving up of the countryside into exclusive parcels:

> Fence now meets fence in owners
>   little bounds
> Of field and meadow large as garden
>   grounds
> In little parcels little minds to please
> With men and flocks imprisoned ill
>   at ease.

He likened the changes to a Napoleonic invasion, levelling every bush, tree and hill. However, in 'The Fallen Elm' it was the effect on ordinary people that unleashed his rage:

> Thus came inclosure – ruin was
>   its guide,
> But freedom's clapping hands
>   enjoyed the sight
> Though comfort's cottage soon
>   was thrust aside
> And workhouse prisons raised
>   upon the site.

William Wordsworth (1770–1850) lived in the Lake District at a time when three-quarters of the land was sheep pasture. Unlike Clare, who grieved over the loss of commons with fatalistic resignation, Wordsworth actually cast down a wall built across a common and led a successful campaign to oppose enclosure near his home. In his poems 'Benjamin the Waggoner' and 'An Evening Walk', Wordsworth talks about Dunmail Raise, a huge cairn of stones situated on the historic boundary between Cumberland and Westmorland, and reputedly the burial place of King Dunmail who died in AD 945. It adjoins the great commons of Helvellyn and Grasmere, which Wordsworth helped to save, ensuring that the land was kept open for the commoners to exercise their rights of 'foddering and goosage'.

All that remains of John Clare's beloved Langley Bush in Northamptonshire today.

The ancient stone cairn of Dunmail Raise near Helvellyn, which features in Wordsworth's poems and adjoins the commons he helped to save.

A Future For Our Commons

Port Meadow remains an important amenity for the people of Oxfor

Commons are an enduring part of the British landscape. They may stretch back to the dawn of farming itself, when early shepherds shared extensive communal pastures and then feasted at great camps that survive as earthen monuments today. In a few cases commons could be direct survivors of such prehistoric systems. However, this should not be overstated. Most of the vast common land which extended across England and Wales in the Middle Ages was lost as local people were cleared from it. Now just a tiny proportion remains. Yet this has more public importance than any other farmland. It is vital for wildlife, archaeology, water supply and tourism. It is closely linked with art, literature, folklore and culture and is all available for public access and enjoyment. It is remarkable that some three-quarters of all our common land is recognised as being nationally or internationally important for its environmental value.

Those commons that have managed to survive are now legally protected from further loss. What threatens commons today is not enclosure, but the demise of tradition. It is a paradox that increasing awareness of the importance of commons coincides with the loss of those cultural traditions which established them in the first place. Fewer people now exercise their common rights, and the number of farmers grazing commons has declined dramatically. Hill farming in particular is a hard life for limited financial reward, even though those who undertake it have long-standing pride in their traditions. Younger generations are often less willing to assume the mantle. However, the decline in commoning affects the lowlands too, and indeed is part of a trend sweeping across Europe. In south-eastern England especially, and also in some parts of Yorkshire and in Wales, almost no practising commoners remain. Certain commons have been neglected for more than a century. As they become overgrown, access is more difficult, wildlife declines and they are vulnerable to fire.

Although commons have changed, they retain many characteristics from their genesis which help make them distinct. First, many people share an interest in them and have a concern for their future. Second, they provide a sense of freedom that comes from their open and unfenced topography. And third, even though they are often nationally important, their care is undertaken by local people. It is in the hands of communities that the future of our common land lies, including both the traditional commoners who have farmed the land for centuries and those who love commons for other reasons, and who all deserve a say in their future.

Selborne in Hampshire, where the common is more overgrown than when described by Gilbert White in the 18th century; the old cricket field on the common is covered in gorse.

Near Coniston. Hill farming is a way of life under threat.

'We shall not cease from exploration' (T.S. Eliot). Cefn Bryn Common on the Gower Peninsula. © Philip Rawnson.

Local residents enjoying a show of orchids at Bromyard Downs Common in Herefordshire.

Even though everyone is within striking distance of a common, it can be frustratingly difficult to identify common land on maps. Sometimes place names have retained the word 'common' for centuries after enclosure. In England and Wales commons form part of 'access land' mapped under the Countryside and Rights of Way Act 2000. This is shown on Ordnance Survey's Explorer series, although these do not distinguish between common land and open country (mountain, moor, heath and down). Online maps of common land are available on www.magic.gov.uk.

Further information can be found online by putting 'Access to the Countryside' and 'Right to Roam' into search engines. Areas which have wider access rights, including for horse-riding (called 'section 15 land' in the Countryside and Rights of Way Act), can also be found through these sites. Many of the largest areas

of common land are within national parks, and information is available on websites.

Many conservation charities seek to protect and manage common land. Britain's oldest conservation charity, the Open Spaces Society (founded 1865), works to protect rights on commons, greens and paths in England and Wales. It has useful information, including practical guides and an explanation of the complex laws concerning commons, on its website: www.oss.org.uk. Publications of particular importance include 'A Common Purpose' – a guide to agreeing management on common land, and 'Finding Common Ground' – a guide to taking account of local community interests in commons.

The Foundation for Common Land promotes traditional management and commoning for the benefit of